Jails in America
An Overview of Issues

Second Edition

Gary Cornelius

ACA Staff:

Bobbie L. Huskey, President

James A. Gondles, Jr., Executive Director

Gabriella Daley, Director, Communications and Publications

Leslie Maxam, Assistant Director, Communications and Publications

Alice Fins, Publications Managing Editor

Michael Kelly, Associate Editor

Mike Selby, Production Editor

Cover art is an architectural drawing for a jail in Manhattan, NY.

Cover art by Graphic Mac, Washington, D.C.

Production by Morgan Graphics, Takoma Park, Maryland

Printed in the U.S.A. by Graphic Communications, Inc., Upper Marlboro, Maryland

This publication may be ordered from:

American Correctional Association

4380 Forbes Boulevard

Lanham, MD 20706-4322

1-800-ACA-JOIN

Library of Congress Cataloging-in-Publication-Data:

Cornelius, Gary F.

Jails in America: an overview of issues / Gary Cornelius. — 2nd ed.

p.   cm

Includes bibliographical references.

ISBN 1-56991-053-7 (pbk.)

1. Jails—United States—History. 2. Jails—United States—Administration. I. Title.

HV9466.C65 1996

365'.34—dc20   96-25771

                                                                                              CIP

Jails in America

INTRODUCTION

We are pleased to provide you with an introductory text on jails. This concise guide presents basic information for those interested in how jails operate and the issues they face. It is intended as a resource to be used for basic information. It succinctly presents the facts and figures on what jails are, types of jails, their costs, and characteristics of their populations. It also offers short accounts of the major issues impacting jails: crowding, legal and medical concerns, and management issues.

In this latter category, the author, Gary Cornelius, a well-respected member of the Fairfax County, Virginia, Sheriff's Office, describes how to handle special populations: substance abusers, the mentally impaired, suicidal inmates, as well as juveniles, women, handicapped, and the elderly. He also introduces the issues of treatment programs, staff training, and alternatives to incarceration, including community corrections and boot camps. The glossary at the end provides short definitions of the common terms used in discussing jails.

Modern jail management requires a well-trained staff who can handle the complexities of managing a crowded facility within the constraints of the law. Increasingly, localities are looking for alternatives to incarceration and alternative management strategies. In today's environment, jail management is no easy challenge. We applaud the hard working men and women who staff our nation's jails.

The American Correctional Association, since 1870 has been in the vanguard of those seeking better and more humane conditions in our penal institutions. As an association, we produce many books, videos and courses, to aid those in the correctional field to achieve a higher level of personal and professional understanding and competence in the performance of their duties. We welcome input from members and invite those nonmembers to join with us to advance the goals of the corrections profession.

James A. Gondles, Jr.
Executive Director
American Correctional Association

ACKNOWLEDGMENTS

For photographs, we appreciate the help of the staff of the Clarke-Frederick-Winchester Regional Adult Detention Center, especially Superintendent Fred Hildebrand and Sergeant Patty Barr, and the staff at the Prince William-Manassas Regional Adult Detention Center, especially Major George Murphy.

We also wish to thank: San Joaquin County, California for the photo on page 8; the Community Relations Service of the United States Department of Justice for the photo on page 14; Dauphin County Prison for the photo on top of page 47; and the Orange County, Florida jail for the photos on the bottom of page 47.

CHAPTER 1

What Is A Jail?

One of the most frequently asked questions is "what is a jail?" This chapter defines the term "jail" and explains the differences between a jail, a prison, and a lockup.

Jails

A jail is a confinement facility which is usually administered and operated by a local law enforcement agency, such as a county sheriff's office or county department of corrections. Jails are intended to confine adults, but may hold juveniles.

The functions of a jail are to:

- Detain offenders who are awaiting trial. These offenders are known as "pretrial detainees." Detention occurs after the offender has been arrested and charged, but before a trial is held to determine guilt or innocence. These people are awaiting their first court appearance, bail or a bond to be set and made, their trial, or for release on their own recognizance pending trial.

- Hold offenders after adjudication who have been sentenced to short periods of confinement, generally to terms of one year or less. These offenders, or inmates, usually are convicted of a minor crime, such as a misdemeanor or nonviolent felony.

- Hold convicted inmates pending their transfer to state or federal departments of corrections or prisons.

- Hold mentally ill inmates who are awaiting transfer to state mental hospitals or substance abusers who are awaiting placement in alcohol/drug treatment facilities.

- Hold juveniles under certain conditions, such as per court order or because the jurisdiction has no juvenile facilities (Allen et al. 1995).

- Hold probation and parole violators awaiting hearings.

- Hold federal prisoners who are awaiting pickup by United States Marshals.

- Hold inmates on outstanding warrants (detainers) from other jurisdictions.

Prisons

A prison is not the same as a jail. A prison is a confinement facility for persons sentenced as adults and is administered, operated, and funded by a state government or the United States government. A prison holds convicted offenders who are sentenced to incarceration terms of more than one year for serious crimes, usually felonies. People in local facilities are "jailed," and people in state and federal institutions are "imprisoned."

Lockups

Another type of confinement facility is the lockup. A lockup is a temporary holding facility, which is usually operated by a police department. Lockups are generally located in police stations/headquarters or in a designated area of the jail building. Lockups have several functions:

- Hold arrestees for no more than forty-eight hours (excluding weekends and holidays) until they are taken before a magistrate, a judge, or are released
- Hold inebriated people until they "sober up" or "dry out"
- Hold juveniles until their parents can be contacted or another placement in a shelter or juvenile detention center can be arranged

There are more than 15,000 lockups in jurisdictions across the United States. Little is known about their size, conditions, staffing, or the types of prisoners they hold.

Jails may be known locally as a house of corrections, county prison, adult detention center, detention center, or correctional facility/institution. Jails are called "prisons" in Pennsylvania. The six states that operate a combined jail/prison system are Delaware, Alaska, Hawaii, Rhode Island, Vermont, and Connecticut.

The History of United States Jails

The word "jail" comes from the Old English word "gaol" (also pronounced jail). In 1166, King Henry II of England initiated the Assize or Constitution of Clarendon. This law established the first gaols which were locally administered and operated. Gaols housed the "misfits" of society. Early gaol populations consisted of paupers, drunkards, prostitutes, thieves, robbers, orphaned children, and debtors, as well as persons who did not agree with the powerful Church of England (Champion 1990).

The "shire-reeves," now known as sheriffs, controlled gaols in their individual shires or localities. Each sheriff had the responsibility for establishing a jail. The individual style of jails carried over to colonial America and continues today. Similarly, today, politics influences the development and operation of U.S. jails. Sheriffs are elected officers, and they bring their own philosophies and staffs to their administrations.

Early English jails held wrongdoers who were accused of violating the law. These violators were held in gaols until court convened and determined the actual punishment. Early jails operated on a fee system. Prisoners had to pay fees to the sheriffs and the gaol keepers.

Jail inmates provided cheap labor. Workhouses, such as Bridewell in 1557, used inmates to work for merchants. Corruption was commonplace; food, sanitation, and medical care were substandard. Conditions in gaols were appalling. In 1724, an inmate described London's Newgate Gaol as a "terrible stinking dark and dismal place" where prisoners endured "great miseries and hardships" (Fox and Stinchcomb 1994). In colonial America, jails continued to be financed by the fee system. Conditions were bad. Many jails held all types of offenders together in dormitories, regardless of gender, age, or type of offense.

Because of the miserable conditions of jails, several reform efforts arose. In 1777, John Howard, a sheriff of Bedfordshire, England, wrote *The State of Prisons*. This essay urged prison and gaol reform, including: improved sanitation, abolition of fees, humane treatment, good character and morals of gaolors, and systematic inspections. As a result of Howard's efforts, Parliament enacted reforms.

In Philadelphia, in 1787, the humane Quaker influence resulted in the formation of the Philadelphia Society for Alleviating the Miseries of Public Prisons (now known as the Pennsylvania Prison Society). Believing that jail conditions needed improvement, these citizen volunteers visited jails bringing food and clothing and providing education and religious instruction.

Also in Philadelphia, in 1790, an institution known as the "first, true correctional institution in America" opened. This was the Walnut Street Jail. Due to the Quaker influence and the ideas of William Penn, the Walnut Street Jail initiated more humane treatment of inmates. Through their efforts, the public and politicians became aware of the bad conditions in jails, and in many cases, improvements occurred. Based on their influence, the Walnut Street Jail separated the more serious prisoners from others; it also separated other prisoners by the seriousness of their offenses *and* by their gender. Prior to this, inmates were all housed together: men, women, and children without any consideration for type of offense. Prisoners engaged in productive labor, and male inmates were paid a daily wage to offset the cost of incarceration. Many prisons were modeled after the concepts of the Walnut Street Jail (Champion 1990).

Since these early jails, jails have had a sketchy but interesting history. Various types of inmate facilities were established. These facilities ranged from sheriffs' homes to barns and small houses. States did not take an interest in jails, and sheriffs were reluctant to share information. In 1880, the United States Census Bureau started compiling information about jails. The Bureau obtained information concerning race, ethnicity, gender, and age every ten years. In 1923, this information was combined into "jail statistics."

In 1923, federal prison inspector Joseph Fishman, in *The Crucible of Crime*, described jail conditions as "horrible" in the 1,500 jails he observed. Recent research indicates that with some exceptions, jail conditions have not changed significantly since Fishman's observations (Thomas 1988, Champion 1990).

In recent decades, jails have undergone the same stresses and strains that have affected prisons—crowding, riots/disturbances, and increasing civil rights' awareness of inmates. Yet, the number of programs for inmates has increased. And, thanks to standards from organizations such as the American Correctional Association and the National Commission on Correctional Health Care, the quality of life in jails for inmates and the working conditions for staff are improving. Those jails that choose to become accredited tend to have better conditions and fewer lawsuits against them.

Population in Jail and Numbers of Jails

From 1880 to 1986, jail population increased from 18,686 to 274,444. Between 1950 and 1986, the jail population in the United States more than tripled. However, between 1970 and 1983, the *number* of jails in the United States decreased (Champion 1990). As of 1993, there were 3,304 jail facilities in the United States. In 1983, there were 3,338 (Bureau of Justice Statistics 1995). These figures *do not* mean that fewer offenders are being incarcerated in jails, nor does it mean that jails are less crowded or being closed for lack of use. This trend does reflect two important facts—many old jails are being closed and a number of small jails are being consolidated into large detention centers or regional jails (Fox and Stinchcomb 1994).

CHAPTER 2

Types of Jails

Jails today are a mixture of large and small facilities. No matter its size, the jail is a central facility of our correctional system. Jails in the United States employ a variety of buildings for many functions. Some jails are used solely for confinement; others house work release programs or operate programs such as house detention.

A significant number of U.S. jails are aging and cannot meet the needs of modern jail operations and the inmate population. According to Fox and Stinchcomb, in 1990, more than 700 jails were over fifty years old. Surprisingly, 140 of those were 100 years old or more!

Many jails in the United States are under construction; this ranges from the building of entire new facilities to renovating existing structures. A 1993 American Jail Association survey of 3,272 jails revealed 177 new facilities under construction and 350 new facilities in the planning stages, but not yet under construction. Thus, 16 percent of the jails surveyed were either being majorly renovated or were planning to expand.

Jails are designed to hold the maximum number of inmates with the minimum number of staff. Jails usually have one of the following three designs:

- **First generation jails:** These are sometimes called "linear." The cells are aligned in rows; the correctional officer walks down a central corridor or catwalk. Interaction with inmates is usually through a food slot or cell bars.

- **Second generation jails**: The officers stay in a central control booth; inmate housing surrounds them. Usual observation is increased, but interaction with inmates is very infrequent.

- **Third generation jails:** Officers are placed inside the housing unit (pod) with no physical barriers. Under this "direct supervision," the officer acts as an inmate behavior manager. The officer has more supervisory authority in the daily operation of the pod.

Direct supervision jail in San Joaquin County, California.

An increasing number of jails are now changing to the direct super-vision model of inmate management. In first and second generation jails, staff *react* to disturbances and problems. In direct supervision, the idea is to prevent problems by actively changing inmate behavior before it erupts into trouble.

CHAPTER 3

Costs of Jails

Ways of estimating or determining jail operating costs vary. Local jails in the United States expended slightly over $9.6 billion from July 1, 1992, to June 30, 1993. This figure is significantly higher than the 1983 total of $2.7 billion. Operating costs such as salaries and wages, employee benefits (contributions by agency), food, supplies, and contractual services (for example, medical and dental services) accounted for 71 percent of expenditures from July 1, 1992 to June 30, 1993. Costs for construction, major repairs, improvements, equipment purchases/repairs, land purchases, and other items accounted for 29 percent of jail expenditures during the same time period (Bureau of Justice Statistics 1995b).

In 1993, the average cost of incarcerating an inmate in jail for one year was $14,667. The average annual cost of housing an inmate in jail rose 57 percent from 1983 to 1993. To further illustrate:

Table 1. Annual Cost per Jail Inmate

		1983	1988	1993
Region:	Northeast	$ 16,657	$ 17,710	$ 22,678
	Midwest	$ 9,020	$ 11,036	$ 15,721
	West	$ 8,310	$ 9,392	$ 14,550
	South	$ 7,185	$ 8,418	$ 11,697
U. S. Average		$ 9,360	$ 10,639	$ 14,667

New York had the highest average operating expenditure per inmate, reported in 1993 ($29,297), and the lowest was Mississippi ($7,014). The average operating cost per inmate *does not* include capital outlays (Bureau of Justice Statistics 1995b).

National Jail Costs

To determine how much it cost the nation to house inmates during 1993, multiply the total average annual cost of $14,667 by the total rated capacity of United States jails, 459,804 beds. The result is almost $6.8 billion.

Alternative Forms of Financing

The escalating costs of jail construction and incarceration have forced local jurisdictions to consider alternative methods of financing. These methods include:

- **General Obligation Bonds.** These bonds, reportedly declining in use, have a twenty-to-thirty-year maturity at a fixed rate. Tax-exempt interest is provided to the investors and approval by voters often is required. These bonds add to the public debt. Usually, new property taxes become sources of payments.
- **Tax-exempt Lease Purchase Bonds.** This type of security raises capital quickly and the source of the lease payments must be identified. Variable rate securities have similar benefits as the fixed rate, but there is a risk of rising interest rates and remarketing. They can be converted to a fixed rate and are only issued in a small number of states.
- **Taxable Private Financing.** This is also called private ownership or privatization. Under this system, the facility is owned by a for profit company or corporation. The owners may receive special tax breaks or advantages and the interest rate for financing by a private company is more costly because a government agency can get a lower interest rate than a private company (National Institute of Justice 1986).
- **Increasing Sales Taxes or Other Taxes.** This creates an increased revenue base from which to obtain funds for construction.
- **Lease/Purchase.** This occurs when the local government obtains funds for jail construction from private firms or investors. By paying an annual sum over a specified number of years, the government leases the facility. At the end of the lease period, the local government assumes ownership. In a variation of this method, the local government creates a nonprofit organization that borrows the money and then the local government may lease the facility from the corporation.
- **State Subsidies for County Jails.** Some states provide subsidies for local corrections— jails, halfway houses, and community corrections facilities. Subsidies also may include funds for jail construction and staff training.
- **Charging Inmates Fees.** In the past several years, jails have started fee systems. Inmates may be required to pay for their incarceration

on a predetermined daily rate. In some jails, inmates are required to pay a fee to obtain the services of the jail's medical staff. Fee systems are used more widely in work release centers because inmates are employed and the costs are deducted from their paychecks. Any jail inmate fee system must take into account inmates who are indigent and cannot pay. Other considerations involve the costs themselves and the avoidance of complaints of economic discrimination when inmates are charged based on their ability to pay.

CHAPTER 4

Characteristics of the Jail Population

The inmates in our nation's jails are a diverse group. Inmates are of various ages, gender, and racial backgrounds. Also, inmates have different criminal histories and various social and economic backgrounds. The following information summarizes the demographics of our jail population:

1. **Sex**: There was a total jail population of 459,804 adult inmates, as of June 30, 1994 (Bureau of Justice Statistics 1995b). In mid-1994, males were 90 percent of the jail population and females were 10 percent.

2. **Race:** The following table shows the race of jail inmates by percentage in midyear 1994 (Bureau of Justice Statistics 1995b):

White: non-Hispanic	39.1
Black: non-Hispanic	43.9
Hispanic	15.4
Others: Asian, Pacific Islander, American Indians, Alaskan Natives	1.6
TOTAL	100%

3. **Age**: In 1991, approximately 33 percent of jail inmates were 18-24 years of age, and almost 43 percent were 25-34 years of age (Bureau of Justice Statistics 1991).

4. **Educational Level**: More than 50 percent of jail inmates had less than a high school education (Allen and Simonsen 1995). Yet, a study of inmates at the Northampton County, Pennsylvania, prison reported (*American Jails* 1994) that inmates' average grade level was tenth grade but their average reading level was at a 5.9 grade level (Gonzales 1994).

Even though jails supply activities, the existence of the inmates is often lonely.

5. **Employment**: Prearrest data showed that 53 percent of jail inmates had full-time employment, 11 percent were working on part-time jobs, while the rate of unemployed inmates was 36 percent (Bureau of Justice Statistics 1991). The average income of inmates who had been free for one year before being jailed was $7,500.00 (Allen and Simonsen 1995). Other research at several California jails indicated that over half of their inmates were unemployed at the time of their jailing and that inmates who were working usually held blue-collar or laborer-type jobs (Jackson 1991).

6. **Marital Status**: Only 19 percent of jail inmates were married.

7. **Substance Abuse**: Historically, jail inmates have displayed high rates of substance abuse. Almost 78 percent of jail inmates had used illegal drugs, and over 27 percent were under the influence of drugs at the time they committed their crime (Bureau of Justice Statistics 1991). Approximately 12 percent were under the influence of both

Inmates meet with staff counselor from the Community Relations Service (CRS) of the United States Department of Justice at the Carl Robinson Correctional Institution in Connecticut. CRS works to lower racial tension by providing prevention, conciliation, and mediation services as well as training for corrections officers at both jails and prisons.

drugs *and* alcohol, while 15.4 percent of the inmates were only under the influence of drugs, and an additional 29.2 percent were under the influence of alcohol only (Bureau of Justice Statistics 1991). More information about substance abuse is in Chapters 7 and 8.

8. **Prior Histories of Arrest and Incarceration**: Most jail inmates are not strangers to the criminal justice system. More than three-fourths of jail inmates had prior sentences of either probation or incarceration. At the time of arrest, about 46.5 percent of jail inmates were on bail, on probation, on parole, or in another type of criminal justice status (Bureau of Justice Statistics 1991).

9. **Types of Offenses**: Almost 23 percent of inmates were incarcerated for violent offenses, such as murder, rape, or robbery. Property crimes accounted for 30 percent, drug offenses for 23 percent, and public order offenses (traffic charges, public intoxication) accounted for about 23 percent of the reasons for incarceration. Approximately one out of every four jail inmates is jailed due to a drug offense (Bureau of Justice Statistics 1991).

10. **Convicted/Unconvicted Status**: Out of 455,500 inmates in jail in 1993, 226,600 had been convicted and 228,900 were unconvicted (Bureau of Justice Statistics 1995b).

11. **Average Length of Sentence/Stay**: In 1988 and 1992, felons who were sentenced to local jails received a sentence of about seven months (Bureau of Justice Statistics 1995b). The average length of stay among pretrial detainees was 67 days and 143.8 days for sentenced inmates. The average for all inmates was 85.8 days (Camp and Camp 1995).

CHAPTER 5

Jail Crowding

The most serious problem facing jail administrators and their staffs is crowding—where to put the large number of offenders being admitted into our nation's jails (Bureau of Justice Statistics 1995).

- In 1993, 13,245,000 offenders were admitted into U.S. jails. This figure includes new admissions (following arrest or court), transfers from other jails, and readmissions, where an inmate is temporarily released to another law enforcement agency's custody and then readmitted.

- In 1993, new jail admissions totaled 9,796,000.

- In 1983, there were 96 jail inmates per 100,000 United States population; in 1994, there were 188 per 100,000. Between 1983 and 1993, the number of jail inmates increased 106 percent. In mid-1994, one out of every 398 adult citizens in the United States was in a local jail.

- On June 30, 1994, local jails in the United States held 490,442 inmates, with an average daily population of 479,957.

- By 1990, 508 municipal jails were operating under consent decrees or court orders, many of which placed a "cap" or limit on the inmate population (Vandenbraak 1995).

Jail crowding is determined by measuring the rated, operational, and design capacities of jails. These terms are defined as follows:

- **Rated capacity** is the number of inmates or beds assigned by a ratings official in the jurisdiction (Bureau of Justice Statistics 1995c).
- **Operational capacity** is the inmate population at which the jail can safely operate from day to day. For example, a jail with a design capacity of 500 double cells which has inmates sleeping in living

areas or dayrooms on bunk beds may house another 250 inmates. The operational capacity is 750. The jail administrator, warden, or agency head (sheriff) usually is responsible for deciding what the operational capacity is. In large jails, it is simply how many inmates they are required to hold, while in smaller facilities, it is how many inmates can be effectively and safely managed.

- **Design capacity** is the number of inmates that the planners and architects intended for the facility, or more simply, what the blueprints list.

Ninety-seven percent of United States jail capacity was occupied in 1994 (Bureau of Justice Statistics 1995b). By contrast, in 1983, only 85 percent of jail capacity was occupied; in 1988, it was at 101 percent. Between 1983 and 1993, the number of jail inmates grew at an average yearly rate of 7.5 percent. In mid-1994, U.S. jails had a rated capacity of 504,324 inmates. Even though 97 percent of this was filled, jail space increased 93 percent from 1983 to 1994 (Bureau of Justice Statistics 1995b).

In 1993, the jail population in several states and the District of Columbia exceeded 100 percent of the jail capacity.

State	Jail Capacity Occupied (%) 1993
Virginia	160
South Carolina	124
District of Columbia	121
New Jersey	120
Texas	115
California	113
Massachusetts	106
Washington	102
Pennsylvania	101

In 1994, a survey of 315 jail administrators reported that 35 percent operate jails at over 110 percent capacity. Jails are adding an average of 220 new beds each year (National Institute of Justice 1995).

Jails are of different sizes. The American Correctional Association (1994) reported that there were 3,019 jails in the United States as of December 31, 1992. Jails are divided into four categories based on reported capacity:

Category by Capacity	1992 Total
Mega (1,000+ beds)	67
Large (250-999 beds)	321
Medium (50-249 beds)	1,044
Small (1-49 beds)	1,584

Thirty percent of all jail inmates incarcerated in 1994 were housed in the nation's twenty-five largest jail jurisdictions (Bureau of Justice Statistics 1995b). Los Angeles County, California, with nine facilities, had an average daily population of 19,725 inmates between July 1, 1993 and June 30, 1994. The twenty-five largest jail jurisdictions were in twelve states: California (7), Texas (5), Florida (4) and one each in New York, Illinois, Louisiana, Tennessee, Arizona, Pennsylvania, Maryland, Georgia, and Michigan. The largest individual jail system with fifteen facilities was in New York City (Bureau of Justice Statistics 1995b).

Factors contributing to the growth in the U.S. jail inmate population included:

- increased adult arrest rate
- increased number of jail admissions
- more felons sentenced to local jails
- more inmates arrested and convicted of drug offenses
- increased numbers of inmates held in local jails for crowded state departments of corrections and federal correctional facilities (Bureau of Justice Statistics 1995b)

Due to these increases, jails are crowded. This crowding is exacerbated by at least two other factors:

- Public demand for a "get tough" approach towards offenders manifested by increasing law enforcement expenditures, restricting or abolishing parole in some states, increasing the lengths of sentences for certain crimes, using mandatory sentences, and constructing more correctional institutions. While not all citizens advocate harsh treatment and support alternatives to jail, negative public attitudes often prevail. However, a more realistic view emphasizes the use of community corrections (Welsh 1991).
- Difficulty in choosing sites for new local correctional facilities. This is commonly called the "not in my back yard," or NIMBY impasse. Often, local citizens do not want facilities constructed in their communities. The subsequent delays, meetings, and negotiations between local government and citizens' groups can delay construction projects.

Meanwhile, jails continue to fill up.

Many operations in a jail are affected by crowding. Due to an increased inmate population, departments such as classification, medical, food service, programs, and maintenance face increased workloads. Over 25 percent of the nation's largest jails were under court order in 1991 to limit their jail populations (Allen and Simonsen 1995). Increasing numbers of inmates are housed in a jail, but jail staff levels do not keep pace. This results in stress and tension for both the inmates and staff. According to most jail administrators, when the jail is at 90 percent of capacity, all flexibility, specifically in classification and housing, is lost (Allen and Simonsen 1995).

Alternatives to jail and jail crowding are discussed in chapter 12, "Future Trends in Jails."

The control center runs all security and communications systems of the jail. Here officers from Prince William-Manassas Regional Adult Detention Center in Manassas, Virginia serve during the late night hours.

CHAPTER 6

Legal Issues and Jails

Frequently, lawsuits are filed by inmates against sheriffs, jail administrators, staff members, and officials of local governments. Usually, these lawsuits challenge unconstitutional conditions of incarceration, allege mistreatment of inmates, deliberate indifference and negligence of staff, inadequate supervision, and lack of due process. In 1992, over 42,000 lawsuits were filed against some type of correctional facility, including 10,000 in New York alone (Allen and Simonsen 1995).

In 1993, 413 jurisdictions with large jail populations were under court order citing specific defects in conditions of confinement which had to be corrected; 324 were ordered to limit population. (Bureau of Justice Statistics 1995d). In descending order of severity, these defects or problems included:

- Crowded living units
- Recreational facilities
- Medical services/facilities
- Visitation policies/procedures
- Disciplinary policies/procedures
- Food service
- Administrative segregation policies/procedures
- Staffing patterns
- Grievance policies/procedures
- Training/education programs
- Fire hazards
- Counseling programs
- Classification of inmates
- Library services

Generally, both convicted inmates and pretrial detainees retain important constitutional rights, despite being incarcerated. The court noted in *Wolff v. McDonnell*, 418 U.S. 539 (1974), that "there is no iron curtain between the Constitution and the prisons of this country." This, and other court rulings, apply to both prisons and jails.

These rights are established in the Constitution and the Bill of Rights.

Specific amendments under which inmates have sued include:

First Amendment, which governs inmates' rights to freedom of speech, exercise of religion, access to the press, and the right of correspondence (mail)

Fourth Amendment, which concerns inmates' rights to privacy and guidelines governing searches

Eighth Amendment, which governs what conditions are found to be cruel and unusual punishment and concerns with medical care

Fourteenth Amendment, which states that persons shall not be deprived of due process of law or denied equal protection of the laws (Collins 1993)

Inmate lawsuits can be *habeas corpus* actions where the inmate challenges the legality of being in custody; tort suits alleging damage or harm due to negligence; or civil rights actions, where inmates claim that their constitutional rights were violated due to a condition, practice, policy, or procedure in the correctional facility. Most inmate suits are civil rights actions brought under 42 U.S. Code Section 1983, or the Civil Rights Act, passed in 1871. It states that anyone acting under color of law (such as a correctional worker) who deprives a United States citizen of "rights, privileges, or immunities" under the Constitution and laws shall be liable for damages.

One question the courts decided concerned the rights of pretrial detainees compared with the rights of convicted inmates. Pretrial detainees are in jail awaiting trial and are presumed innocent (Fisher 1987). The Supreme Court, in *Bell v. Wolfish*, 441 U.S. 529 (1979), held that due process prohibited the imposition of punishment on pretrial detainees. However, the Court noted that not every condition in the facility is punishment. Inmates must show that for a specific condition to be punitive, they must prove an intent to punish and show that the condition is not related to a legitimate goal, such as maintaining order, security, preventing contraband, and so on.

In 1981, in *Rhodes v. Chapman*, 101 S.Ct. 2392 (1981), the Supreme Court ruled that double celling or double bunking of inmates was not unconstitutional and not cruel and unusual punishment. To be punitive, the authorities must wantonly inflict pain on inmates by, for example, depriving them of food, decreasing their medical care, or lowering sanitation standards (Champion 1990).

Medical Care

All jail and prison inmates are entitled to adequate medical care at the same levels of treatment as citizens on the outside would receive. In the 1976 case, *Estelle v. Gamble*, 97 S.Ct. 285 (1976), the Supreme Court said that to constitute cruel and unusual punishment, inmates must show that the failure to provide adequate medical care was due to "deliberate indifference" to serious medical needs. Deliberate indifference, for example, means that a key part of a health care delivery system is missing or the response to a serious medical need is either extremely inadequate or nonexistent, or the staff knew of a dangerous condition and ignored it or did little or nothing to correct the problem.

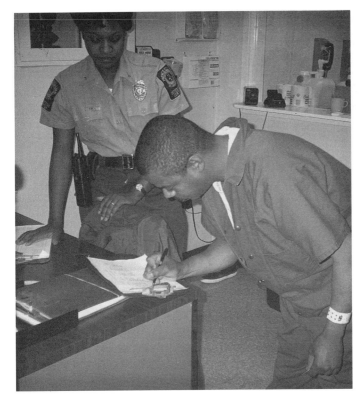

Inmates are required to sign documentation that they receive their property.

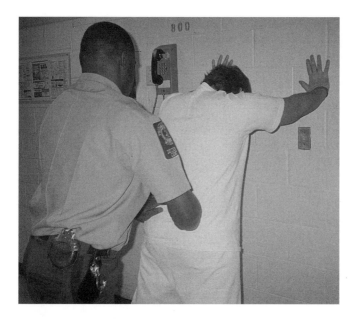

Jail inmates may be searched randomly at any time for contraband.

Personal and Property Searches

Searches are essential for maintaining security in jails. The Fourth Amendment's protections against unreasonable searches are decreased, but not eliminated, for inmates. Cells may be randomly searched without the inmate being present. Pat-downs and urine tests (also viewed as searches) may be performed randomly. Strip searches can be conducted of all inmates following their opportunity to obtain contraband. Most jails have policies that allow strip searches based on reasonable suspicion. Body cavity searches may be necessary but have to be based on reasonable cause. These searches should be conducted by the jail's medical staff in private (Collins 1993). Courts have held that arrestees may only be strip searched upon reasonable suspicion and that policies which require all arrestees to be strip searched are unconstitutional (Collins 1993).

Cruel and Unusual Punishment

Inmates have used lawsuits under the Eighth Amendment to attack jail conditions. The cases of *Bell v. Wolfish* and *Rhodes v. Chapman* established the fact that crowded jails are not necessarily unconstitutional. In *Wilson v. Seiter*, 111 S.Ct. 2321 (1991), the Supreme Court ruled that plaintiffs, or inmates, must prove that the conditions of the facility must be extremely bad and fail to provide one or mo. basic human needs, and the defendants, or staff, knew of these bad conditions and failed to correct them (deliberate indifference). These "basic human needs" are adequate food, adequate clothing, shelter (physical plant), sanitation, accessible and competent medical care, and personal safety—protection from rape, assault, or serious injury (Collins 1993).

Equal Access to Programs

Female inmates must be provided the same access to programs as male inmates, according to the courts. Recently, courts have ruled that programs and facilities for women must be generally equivalent to those programs and services provided for men. These cases concern the Equal Protection Clause of the Fourteenth Amendment (Collins and Hagar 1995).

Due Process

In 1996, Congress passed the Prison Litigation Reform Act, which tries to limit the power of federal courts to order relief of large jail or prison cases. It demands that inmates pay the costs of filing fees and other costs. However, it may be held unconstitutional.

The landmark federal case of *Wolff v. McDonnell*, 418 U.S. 539 (1974), established the requirement for a hearing over rules' violations where the loss of good time may be involved. The Court ruled that the following elements had to be included in the hearing process:

- a hearing, at which the accused inmate has the right to be present
- advance, written notice of the changes provided to the inmate at least twenty-four hours before the hearing
- opportunity for the inmate to present evidence on his/her behalf, including calling witnesses
- assistance from another inmate or staff person
- impartial hearing
- written decision: guilt or innocence and the evidence relied on for the decision

Inmates may appeal a guilty decision to a higher authority. In cases of administrative segregation, the inmates must be told of the reason for such placement, be given an opportunity to respond, and their status must be reviewed periodically. Many institutions hold formal administrative hearings to satisfy this requirement (Collins 1993).

In June 1995, in *Sandin v. Connor*, 115 S.Ct. 2293, the Supreme Court initiated a new test of due process rights in which the key factor is the seriousness of the inmate's loss, not the mandatory language of the institution's rules. This new standard infers due process rights created by the state (jail/prison) only when the punishment imposes a "significant hardship on the inmate in relation to the ordinary incidents of prison life." It is not clear yet how this ruling will affect an inmate's rights to due process (for example, the right to call witnesses, appeal and other issues). Experts anticipate that inmate litigation will help clarify this decision.

Although attorneys file many civil rights actions on behalf of inmates, many are filed by "jailhouse lawyers." These inmates generally are self-taught in legal matters, and not only file lawsuits, but assist other inmates with their cases or lawsuits. Using law libraries, whose use has been supported by the courts, these inmates act as their own lawyers. Many Section 1983 lawsuits are dismissed for several reasons: the plaintiff fails to comply with court rules, there is no evidence of a constitutional rights violation, or it is a frivolous action. However, many Section 1983 suits do make it to court.

Type of Section 1983 Suits Filed (by percentage)

Physical security (failure to protect)	21
Medical treatment	17
Due process (improper disciplinary hearings, etc.)	13
Challenges to conviction (invalid sentence, etc.)	12
Miscellaneous (denial of parole and other reasons)	10
Physical conditions (inadequate sanitation, crowding, and other issues)	9
Denial of access to courts or attorneys	7
Living conditions (inadequate clothing or other issues)	4
Denial of religious expression, visits, racial discrimination	4
Assault by arresting officer	3
TOTAL	100%

Source: Hansen and Daley 1995

In determining the constitutionality of jails, generally courts have looked for such things as: proper sanitation; provision of health, medical, and mental health services; substance abuse treatment programs; educational programs; outdoor recreation; indoor activities; work opportunities; law and recreational libraries; religious programs; commissary; visitation opportunities; and work release options.

Federal Laws

Corrections legal experts predict that in the 1990s, more inmate lawsuits will involve interpretations of federal statutes, and not necessarily the United States Constitution (Collins and Hagar 1995). Two recent federal laws that are resulting in many lawsuits include the Americans with Disabilities Act (ADA) and the Religious Freedom Restoration Act (RFRA).

Passed in 1990, the Americans with Disabilities Act provides protections for disabled inmates and staff who receive government services, programs, or activities, including those provided in a local jail. For inmates with disabilities, this Act requires changes in the physical plant (such as the addition of wheelchair ramps and handrails) and changes in procedures and programs that require accommodating disabled inmates, including provision of accessible housing or work.

The Religious Freedom Restoration Act also has an impact on local jails. Until this law was passed, jail administrators easily could restrict inmates' abilities to practice their religion, due to the courts deferring to their judgments on security matters. Under the Religious Freedom Restoration Act, security matters must be more convincingly demonstrated, and the courts can "second guess" jail administrators about available alternatives to accommodate an inmate's religious practices. For example, if an inmate's faith requires a special service and items and there is no room available, the jail may have to allow the service in the inmate's cell and supply the necessary items (Collins and Hagar 1995). When deciding freedom of religion issues under the First Amendment, courts will continue to use the "sincerity of belief" test as an indicator if the jail must accommodate the inmate's religious requests (Collins and Hagar 1995).

The Civil Rights of Institutionalized Persons Act (CRIPA), 42 USC 1992, provides that the United States Department of Justice can bring civil rights lawsuits on behalf of persons in prisons or jails. While this law is not invoked often, it encourages jails and prisons to initiate grievance procedures. The goal is to reduce the number of inmate lawsuits and have inmate complaints handled by a grievance process. For example, an inmate may say that the medical staff is not treating an ailment. Instead of filing a section 1983 action, the inmate could file a grievance with the jail staff and the problem may be resolved (Collins 1993).

In several cases, the Supreme Court has set forth policy on inmates' access to courts and legal materials. In *Johnson v. Avery*, 393 U.S. 483 (1969), the Court ruled that correctional facilities may impose reasonable restrictions on inmates helping each other, but cannot prohibit such activities. Reasonable restrictions can include security regulations. In *Bounds v. Smith*, 430 U.S. 817 (1977), the Court said that the states had a duty to assist inmates in the preparation and filing of "meaningful legal papers," such as litigation and court motions. Some jails provide law libraries with up-to-date codes and texts. Some jails allow paralegals to assist inmates. Recent federal court cases have ruled that when inmates are denied access to legal materials or a law library, they must prove actual injury or harm in order to make a Constitutional claim (Collins and Hagar 1995). No harm need be shown if the inmate can demonstrate that the jail has no legal materials generally available. A few jails now provide inmate law libraries with legal cases and codes through the use of computers.

CHAPTER 7

Jail Management

Jail staffs must deal with a diverse inmate population. Many have emotional, behavorial, physical and/or psychological problems. These groups include:

- Men and women
- Substance abusers
- Mentally ill/disabled
- Suicidal inmates
- Juveniles
- Assaultive inmates

- Gangs/extremist groups
- Individuals with disabilities
- Individuals in protective custody
- Foreign/ethnic groups
- Individuals with medical problems/HIV
- The elderly

Substance Abusers

Jail inmates have a high rate of illegal substance abuse—drugs and alcohol. Adolescents and young adults are most at risk. Many inmates start out experimenting with drugs and alcohol and become "hooked" with progressive use; 58 percent indicate that they are regular users (Fox and Stinchcomb 1994).

In state courts, from which offenders are sent to local jails, drug offenses accounted for almost a third of felony convictions in 1991. In 1992, in state courts, 42 percent of convicted drug offense felons were sent to prison, 28 percent were sent to jail, and 30 percent received probation (Bureau of Justice Statistics 1994).

Drugs used by inmates (in percentages)
Note: Many inmates used multiple drugs.

Cocaine/crack	55.4%
Amphetamines	22.1%
Marijuana/hashish	20.7%
LSD	18.6%
Heroin	18.2%
PCP	13.9%

Source: Bureau of Justice Statistics 1991

According to Bureau of Justice Statistics data, in 1993, 978 jails reported regular drug testing of inmates: 79 performed mandatory tests, 228 conducted mandatory tests for some inmates, 324 tested randomly, and 701 tested when staff had reasonable suspicion of use. Inmates in 144 jails were tested for other reasons, such as entering work release, returning from a pass/furlough, receiving a court order, entering a trustee (inmate worker) program, or they were tested at the request of a parole/probation officer (Bureau of Justice Statistics 1995d).

For the jail officer, the management of drug abusers is a problem. From July 1992 to June 30, 1993, seventeen jail inmates reportedly died from alcohol or drug overdoses (Bureau of Justice Statistics 1995b). The jail officer must deal with the physical and behavioral effects of drugs. For example, a newly arrived inmate "high" on cocaine has to be observed for physical effects such as convulsions or cardiac arrest. Withdrawal may result in depression, and inmates in a depressed state are prone to suicide.

Urinalysis results from 1991 show that 50 percent of females and 48 percent of males charged with assault tested positive for drugs; for burglary: 68 percent of males and 63 percent of females tested positive; for homicide: 48 percent of males and 65 percent of females; for robbery: 65 percent of males and 76 percent of females (Allen and Simonsen 1995).

In 1989, 41.3 percent of jail inmates reported being under the influence of alcohol at the time of the offense; 20.9 percent said they were alcoholics. About a third of the jail inmates had participated in a prior substance abuse program.

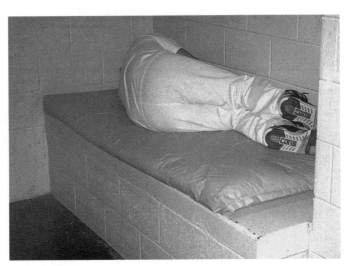

Many jail inmates have problems ranging from physical illness, to substance abuse withdrawal, to depression.

Due to the impairment of the central nervous system, the alcohol abusing offender must be carefully watched by the jail officer. Alcohol results in impaired judgment, release of inhibitions, loss of balance, and stupor. Inmates under its influence cannot perform normal critical thinking and can be hard to handle, belligerent, and loud. The jail officer must be concerned if the inmate has ingested both drugs and alcohol. Alcohol abusers in jail have to be carefully observed and *not* just put into a cell to "sleep it off." An inmate might get delirium tremens or "the DTs" during alcohol withdrawal. The DTs involve tremors, hallucinations, delusions, and seizures in the later stages.

Mentally Disordered

Offenders with symptoms of mental illness often enter our nation's jails. Mentally ill offenders present several problems to jail staffs: their dealing with the stress of confinement; the potential of danger to themselves, other inmates, and the jail staff; and the possibility that if not handled properly or untreated, the symptoms of their mental illness may worsen (Veysey et al. 1995). Mentally ill offenders have different degrees of mental illness ranging from psychosis to emotional disruptions or dysfunction in their abilities to work or relate to other people. Mentally ill offenders are not necessarily violent and are no more at risk than the outside population of acting violently (Veysey et al. 1995).

In 1992, the National Alliance for the Mentally Ill published a report which said that:

- On any given day, 86 percent of our nation's jails hold mentally ill individuals
- Over 30,700 seriously mentally ill individuals serve time in our nation's jails every day
- Approximately one third of 1,391 jails surveyed report holding mentally ill people without pending charges

Approximately 600,000 mentally ill people are among the 7 million people jailed in county and city jails annually (Judiscak 1995).

In jails and lockups, the most important issues are safety and stability. Offenders who are mentally ill must be identified by routine screening, followed up by evaluations by qualified mental health staff. For this group, stabilization by crisis intervention, medication, and frequent staff contact is crucial (Veysey et al. 1995).

While mentally ill offenders are arrested and incarcerated for a variety of crimes, jails report the most common offenses for which they are incarcerated include (Trupin 1993):

Most Common Offenses (in percentage)
Note: Offenders may fall into more than one category.

Assault and/or battery	41
Theft	30
Disorderly conduct	29
Drug and alcohol offenses	29

Jails also house developmentally disabled inmates—inmates who are functionally illiterate, mildly retarded, have learning disabilities, a low intellectual ability, lack social or life skills, or exhibit organic brain disorders. Estimates are that 3 to 10 percent of the general inmate population are developmentally disabled and exhibit a reduced capacity to comprehend their charges, their sentences, and how to deal with being incarcerated. An estimated 42 to 50 percent of jail inmates are functionally illiterate, even though many have been graduated from high school. In a South Carolina study, seven out of forty-five mentally retarded inmates referred for evaluation did not know what "guilty" meant (Jones 1995).

Because of the requirements of the Americans with Disabilities Act, corrections facilities must provide mental health screening, evaluation, and treatment to inmates with mental disabilities, including those with developmental or psychological disorders, retardation, organic brain syndrome, emotional illness, or a specific learning disability.

Suicidal Inmates

Jail staffs must be alert for inmates who exhibit depression or are in crises which may lead to suicidal behavior. In 1993, suicides were the second leading cause of death in local jails, and 234 jail inmates killed themselves (Bureau of Justice Statistics 1995b). Inmates under the influence of drugs/alcohol when they were admitted committed 60 percent of the suicides. Most suicides in correctional facilities are by hanging

(Rowan 1991). Lawsuits filed by suicide survivors are common. To defend against them, jail staffs must take preventative measures. (See Drapkin, *Developing Policies and Procedures for Jails* 1996).

Suicide Prevention Policies	Number of Jails
Jails with no suicide prevention policy	317
Jails with a suicide prevention policy	2,628
Jails with staff suicide prevention training	1,796
Jails with risk assessment at intake	2,209
Jails with "suicide watch" cell (including checks every 10-15 minutes)	2,025
Live or remote monitoring	1,801
Special counseling (mental health staff, etc.)	1,885
Inmate suicide prevention teams	120
Other methods (removal of belts, shoe laces, issue paper gowns, transfer to psychiatric ward, etc.)	53

Bureau of Justice Statistics 1995d

Juveniles

Juveniles, as defined by most states, are persons under the age of eighteen who are subject to the jurisdiction of a juvenile court. In 1994, 6,725 jail inmates were under eighteen years of age; 76 percent of those were juveniles who were tried as or were pending trial as adults.

Occasionally, under laws and rules of some courts, juveniles can be held in a local jail. If juveniles are accused of a serious crime and are certified by a court to stand trial as adults, they can be held in a local jail. This also applies if the juvenile is sentenced as an adult.

Juveniles accused of actions which would be crimes if they were adults also can be held in local jails. Generally, they must be separated by sight and sound from the general adult inmate population. Some jurisdictions limit the time that a juvenile can be jailed to less than six hours. However, laws allowing juveniles to be treated as adults are becoming more common nationwide.

Many adult jails do not have sufficiently trained staff, health, and recreational facilities, or programs to adequately house juveniles. Young "first time" offenders may be victimized by hard core, aggressive juveniles or others. The rate of juvenile suicides in adult jails is almost eight times higher than juvenile suicides in juvenile detention centers (Fox and Stinchcomb 1994).

Most juvenile offenders who are confined are in institutions specifically designed and operated for juveniles. In 1993, approximately 96,000 juvenile offenders were in public or private juvenile detention and correctional facilities. Also, in 1993, the average daily population of juveniles in local jails was 3,400, up markedly from 1,760 in 1983 (Bureau of Justice Statistics 1995b).

In 1974, the Federal Juvenile Justice and Delinquency Prevention Act restricted the jailing of juveniles in adult jails to limited situations. Subsequent amendments made exceptions for short-term detentions if juveniles and adults were kept separate. As a result of sight and sound restrictions, juveniles frequently were placed in solitary confinement (Kerle 1991). Jails face serious liability issues when juveniles are jailed in adult facilities—lawsuits are filed when juveniles are injured or commit suicide (Dale 1991). Some states have enacted plans to phase out the placement of juveniles in adult jails.

Women

Female inmates are 10 percent of the jail population. In 1993, there were 22,700 convicted females and 21,300 unconvicted females in U. S. jails (Bureau of Justice Statistics 1994). Also in 1993, almost 3 million females were arrested—about 19.5 percent of the total number of arrests (Bureau of Justice Statistics 1994). Not all arrests result in time in jail. Some offenders enter prison and some are placed on probation. Others enter a diversion program or a community corrections program in lieu of incarceration. Males are imprisoned at a rate about eighteen times higher than females.

According to 1993 arrest statistics, females were arrested mostly for arson, theft, aggravated assault, other assaults (misdemeanors), embezzlement, prostitution, driving while intoxicated, and disorderly conduct. Drug offenses among female arrestees are high, almost 158,000 in 1993 (Bureau of Justice Statistics 1994). During the 1980s, there was a 138 percent increase in the number of women incarcerated in local jails. Almost half of this startling increase was due to females being jailed for drug offenses.

Overall, 76 percent of women prisoners in correctional facilities are mothers; many are single parents. Many female inmates are young, unmarried, and less likely to have a high school education or be employed prior to their arrest than their male counterparts (Fox and Stinchcomb 1994). Due to the separation from the children, inmate mothers can suffer depression, which adds to the stress of incarceration. The National Council on Crime and Delinquency estimated that on any given day in 1991, 167,000 children had mothers who were in jail or prison (Ragghianti 1994).

Research by the American Correctional Association found that the typical female inmate has an extensive history of drug/alcohol abuse, usually starting around age thirteen. Depression and suicide attempts are prevalent in this group. A female inmate is three times more likely than a male inmate to have suffered physical or sexual abuse (Ragghianti 1994). The number of female inmates with a severe mental disability is estimated at 13 percent (Rubin and McCampbell 1995).

Many jails offer substance abuse and rehabilitation programs for females, including programs that allow them to spend time with dependent children, and many offer parenting courses. Programs such as STEP (Self Taught Emprovement and Pride) at Rikers Island, New York, and Oregon's ADAPT (Alcohol and Drug Abuse Prenatal Treatment) help in rehabilitating jailed females (see also Boudouris 1996).

Operating a control booth requires the ability to communicate to staff clearly and consistently and to be trained for control of emergency situations (Clarke-Frederick-Winchester Regional Adult Detention Center, Winchester, Virginia).

Assaultive Inmates

Almost all jails have rules that prohibit violence. Yet, jail staffs must deal with inmates who are incarcerated against their will and sometimes are resistant to authority or who physically victimize other inmates. Inmate violence also may be a result of mental illness or the effects of drugs and alcohol abuse. Jail inmates can be charged under criminal statutes. Jail officers must be proficient in nonlethal use of force, including "stun" type devices; nonchemical personal defense agents, such as oleoresin capsicum ("pepper") spray, and "hands on" holds such as wrist/arm locks. Violent inmates should be segregated from the general jail population.

Of the 101 jail systems surveyed, 3,162 assaults on staff by inmates were reported and 19,967 assaults by inmates on inmates occurred in 99 jail systems the same year (Camp and Camp 1995). A study of 112 officers at a Pennsylvania county prison in 1990 found that 56 percent had been assaulted at some time in their career and 89 percent had been threatened with physical assault (Jefferis 1994). Crowded institutions, young aggressive inmates, and the negative effects of the jail environment on inmates all increase the likelihood of assault on officers.

Gangs/Extremist Groups

Gangs in U. S. jails in recent years are a critical problem. Most jail gangs originate as street gangs. Many are based on racial or ethnic groups. Often, gangs in jails group together for power (against staff and to victimize inmates) or for protection (from interference from staff or rival gangs). Gang members in jails and prisons engage in assaults, extortion, drug dealing, victimization of nongang inmates, manufacture of contraband, and homicide. Prison/jail gangs engage in antisocial, antiauthority, and criminal behaviors which makes jail operations difficult. Managing inmate gang members requires constant monitoring, information gathering, and decisive action such as segregation, disciplinary action, or filing criminal charges.

Inmates with Disabilities

Jail inmates have many types of disabilities. Inmates with physical disabilities who are admitted to jail must be kept safe, comfortable, and have their basic needs met. Inmates who are in wheelchairs, use crutches/walkers, or who are handicapped physically (such as amputees) must be housed in ways that the staff can observe them, be responsive to their needs, or evacuate them in case of an emergency, such as a fire. The Americans with Disabilities Act (ADA) specifies that common-use areas in a jail, such as exercise areas, workshops, classrooms, cafeterias, or any room/space for inmates' use must be accessible to everyone including disabled inmates.

According to ADA regulations, effective September 1996, at least 3 percent of inmate cells must be accessible, and there must be at least one cell for protective custody, disciplinary segregation, substance abuse detox, or medical isolation. These regulations also cover visiting, bathing, toilets, the hearing impaired, cell storage areas, seating, and other areas.

The ADA also requires that inmates with disabilities have equal access to a jail's programs and services by jail staff so that all areas are "readily accessible and usable" by inmates with disabilities. In summary, inmates and visitors must be afforded access to programs, services, and activities to which nondisabled inmates and visitors have access. This requirement applies to alterations of existing structures and new construction (Thompson and Ridlon 1995).

Protective Custody

Occasionally in jails, certain inmates may need to be placed in protective custody—housing them individually away from the jail's general population. Protective custody inmates are on administrative segregation; they generally have the same rights and receive the same privileges as general population inmates.

An American Correctional Association study found that corrections staff estimated the following percentage of inmates in their facilities on protective custody for the following reasons (in percentage):

- They are thought to be informers   32
- They need protection from retaliation
  (arguments, bad debts, and other concerns)   29
- They need protection from sexual assault   16
- They are mentally disturbed   5
- They want to avoid work   7
- Other, miscellaneous   10

(American Correctional Association 1983)

Due to the absence of social interaction and normal, daily activity, inmates in protective custody should be frequently observed for signs of physical and mental health decline.

Foreign/Ethnic Groups

Offenders admitted to jail may come from various foreign/ethnic groups. Many foreign-born inmates speak little or no English. Since some gangs are formed along ethnic lines, staff must take care not to house gang members together. One method of improving communications with foreign-born offenders is to have the jail rules and regulations published in various languages. Interpreters from the jail staff, the courts, or approved volunteers, also can assist. Programs in foreign languages also are beneficial. Foreign inmates may be subject to harassment and prejudice from other inmates. In mid-1994, an estimated 75,500 Hispanic inmates (15.4 percent) and 7,700 inmates (1.6 percent) from other races (Asians, Pacific Islanders, American Indians, and Alaskan natives) were jailed in the United States (Bureau of Justice Statistics 1995b).

Medical Problems/HIV

Offenders entering jails generally have followed a lifestyle of poor diet and drug and alcohol abuse. As a result, they lack good dental hygiene, have poor hygiene practices, and have poor health. Jail medical staffs must screen offenders, obtain a medical history, and make decisions concerning basic treatment. Hepatitis A and B, HIV infection, measles, and drug-resistant tuberculosis are among the jail population's medical problems. Jail medical staffs conduct sick calls and treat these problems: colds, viruses, skin infections, stomach problems, and others. Well-managed jails employ the services of a medical doctor who may see inmates daily or several times per week. Medical costs include salaries, the cost of hospitalization in serious medical cases or pregnancy, as well as the costs for illness, injury, pharmaceuticals, medical equipment, and basic dental care.

In 1993, about 1.8 percent of inmates in local jails were HIV positive, and in the nation's fifty largest jails, almost 3 percent of inmates were HIV positive. In 1993, AIDS deaths accounted for 9.7 percent of the total deaths of jail inmates (Bureau of Justice Statistics 1994).

Unfortunately, HIV infection has been a contributing factor in the rise of multiple drug resistant (MDR) tuberculosis (TB). Institutionalized environments, such as jails, help the disease flourish and spread. Jails are at extreme risk due to crowding, poor ventilation, and constant movement of inmates to different housing areas. While studies show that inmates are three times more likely to have TB than people in the general population, most jails do not have mandatory screening. Yet, this is changing: TB testing/screening is becoming more widely used (Smith 1994).

Medical Care in Jails

In 1993, out of 3,268 jails surveyed:

No medical facilities	1,670
Jails with medical facilities	1,252
Infirmary: overnight beds	460
Infirmary: no overnight beds	565
Detoxification units	324
Psychiatric units	141
Other: restraints, isolation, pre/postnatal care, dental offices	142

(Bureau of Justice Statistics 1995d)

Elderly Inmates

By 2001, an estimated one out of ten inmates, or about 125,000 inmates, will be over fifty-years old. Contributing to the "aging of inmates" in jails and prisons are longer sentencing and the tightening up or abolition of parole. Elderly inmates pose management problems such as requiring additional health care; special diet needs; and potential victimizing by younger, more aggressive inmates. Also, elderly inmates are prone to depression and hopelessness. Elderly inmates' medical care costs more, including costs for dentures, eyeglasses, cardiac care, and kidney dialysis—these costs may increase fourteen-fold by 2005. Early release, executive clemency, pardon, or alternative housing could be used to cope with this problem (Fox and Stinchcomb 1994).

Dealing With Special Management Problems

Jail staffs are more efficient when they use a "team" approach for special problem inmates. This approach involves:

- **Observation**: Incoming inmates must be observed closely for problems on admission. Substance abusers, mentally ill inmates, and suicidal inmates usually display physical or behavioral signs that alert the officer to observe closely.

Signs of Alcohol/Drug Abuse

- Disorientation
- Confusion
- Delerium
- Poor coordination: cannot stand/walk
- Slurred speech
- Pupils: dilated/pinpoint
- Aggressive behavior
- Restlessness
- Vomiting
- Agitation
- Lethargy
- Rapid/shallow breathing
- Complaints: very hot or cold
- "Tracks"/needle marks
- Odor of alcohol
- Cramps
- Nausea
- Diarrhea

Alcohol/Drug Withdrawal

- Anxiety/fear/being "scared"
- Agitation/excitedness
- Sweating
- Hallucinations
- Vomiting
- Difficulty in breathing
- Tremors/shakes
- Cannot sleep
- Talkative
- Delerium
- Nausea
- Complaints

Signs of Possible Mental Illness

- Inappropriate behavior to situation
- Fear
- Withdrawal
- Feelings of confusion
- Talk of suicide
- Extreme emotions
- Delusions/hallucinations: such as, thinks he/she is a famous person, hears voices, indicates unusual or unreal physical symptoms
- Anxiety
- Depression
- Lack of reality
- Anger
- Mania: nonstop energy
- Any "unusual" or unrealistic behavior: inmate is not "normal"

Signs of Suicidal Behavior

- Depression
- Crying
- Varying moods
- Feelings of self-blame/ worthlessness/guilt
- Threats of suicide
- Suicide attempt
- Tenseness
- Withdrawal/silence

Source: Virginia Office of Forensic Service 1986

Jail staff must be alert for inmate behavior that is not ordinary and medical conditions that require attention, as well as other factors. Information on these issues and other areas of concern can come from arresting police officers, transporting officers, attorneys, and the inmate's family.

• **Documentation**: Staff must document the behavior and symptoms thoroughly, for further use by staff, and as a protection against litigation.

• **Referral**: Problem inmates must be referred to staff such as medical staff or mental health staff who can provide qualified assistance.

The classification section can be described as the "nerve center" of the jail. The process of classifying jail inmates has three major functions:

1. **Assessment of inmates' background and behavior** for assignment to proper custody/supervision levels. This occurs through an intake process to find out the inmate's criminal, social, and medical histories (including prior incarcerations), educational/vocational background, religious preference, mental history, known enemies, suicidal ideation, the instant offense, and family contact.

2. **Development of a program/treatment plan**: the institutional classification committee (ICC) evaluates information. This committee consists of representatives of the classification, mental health, custody, and medical sections, or a unit team. The team determines where the inmates will live, what treatment (usually programs) they will need, and what their work assignments will be. This may be done through subjective means (no fixed rules) or by a predetermined set of scored factors.

3. **Regular, periodic monitoring of the inmate's progress**. Classification staff and the institutional classification committee accomplish this by moving inmates, if necessary, to different locations and custody levels based on inmates' behavior or input from the custody staff. Classification staffs deal with inmate disputes and problems (such as incompatibilities and personal problems) to ensure safety of the staff and inmates (American Correctional Association 1989).

The classification division also handles disciplinary hearings, inquiries from families, attorneys, police, probation/parole, and other jails or prisons. The committee also holds administrative hearings when moving an inmate to a more secure custody level, removing a privilege, or placing an inmate in administrative segregation. In jails having unit management, a team consisting of the unit manager, case manager, counselor(s), educational staff, mental health staff, and security/custody assume the functions of a classification committee.

Classification segregates males from females, juveniles from adults, violent from nonviolent inmates, and special management inmates from the general population. Ideally, pretrial inmates should be segregated from convicted inmates, and the sentenced separated from the unsentenced. Due to today's crowded jails, often, this is not feasible.

Security Problems

For a jail to be secure, correctional staff must prevent escapes, control contraband, and maintain control over the movement and activity of inmates. Security is accomplished by security hardware/devices in the physical plant and the competency of the jail staff (American Correctional Association 1989). Jails should have the following security procedures:

- controlled access/exit. Entrances and exits are controlled by staff through officer presence supplemented by video cameras, passes, and security doors

- patrols in housing areas and the jail's outside perimeter where inmates are observed and the physical plant is inspected, inside and out, for lighting, working devices, and other concerns

- searches of inmates, housing/common areas for contraband—illegal or unau-

Many jails have entry-screening devices such as magnometers or metal detectors

thorized items (including weapons or drugs) *or* an excess of authorized items

• accountability of inmates by counting them, knowing their whereabouts at all times, and safely moving/transferring them

• control of keys, tools, medical supplies, drugs and kitchen utensils

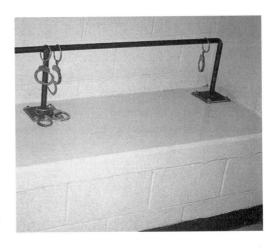

• an inmate identification system: photograph, wristband, or other means that verifies an inmate's identity to staff

• hostage policy that dictates that no inmate will gain release by taking a hostage

• written security procedures, including post orders

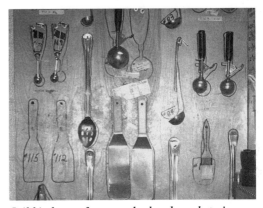

Jail kitchens often use shadow boards to insure proper accounting of utensils. This is essential because utensils can be used as weapons.

Emergencies

Jail emergencies take many forms. They include:

– Riots/disturbances

– Bombs/bomb threats

– Work stoppages: staff and inmate

– Natural disasters: floods, hurricanes, earthquakes, tornadoes

– Hazardous materials spills

– Electrical power failure

– Fires

– Civil disturbances

– Inmate hunger strikes

– Weather emergencies: snowstorms

– Inmate death

– Escapes

(For details on this, see Freeman 1996.)

Jail administrators must rely on their staffs to be proactive. There should be written policies, procedures, and training guidelines to deal with these emergencies. Some emergency conditions—fire hazards, riot-prone climate, escape-risk inmates—have warning signs. Many emergencies, however, such as a bomb explosion, do not.

Often two officers work the control center of a large jail due to the complex security system (Prince William-Manassas Regional Adult Detention Center in Virginia).

Jails should include the following in an emergency plan:

- first response, immediate steps
- primary/secondary steps for resolving the problem
- nonduty chain of command phone numbers and phone numbers of key personnel
- officials authorized to call in outside assistance
- procedures for setting up and operating a command post
- notification points and procedures for reporting problems
- statement of how local agencies can help in an emergency
- provision for staff training in emergency responses and key indicators of potential problems prior to any emergency
- media notification procedures
- method for periodic review of existing procedures

A growing trend in jails is the development of emergency response teams (ERT) that either are part of an on duty shift or are on call to respond in case of emergencies, especially where use of force (such as riots) is involved (Ness 1996 and American Correctional Association 1989).

CHAPTER 8

Treatment Programs
in Jails

Treatment programs for jail inmates involve a variety of options. Treatment programs generally follow the reintegration model of treatment—how to return the offender to his/her community not as an "ex con," but as a responsible, productive citizen who can use community resources to help with problems. Offenders need a means of support and many jail programs can start the process.

Classification helps to identify inmates' problem areas, such as substance abuse. They make referrals to qualified personnel, such as substance abuse counselors or mental health personnel, who can start a treatment plan. Treatment plans include participation in educational, vocational, substance abuse, religious, or social/life skills programs.

Treatment combats "prisonization," a socialization process in which the inmate not only learns the rules of the jail, but also the informal values, customs, and culture of the jail inmate population, including survival skills and how to cope with jail life.

Since 1983, there has been an increase in the number but not the percentage of treatment staff in jails. In 1993, there were 2,100 people

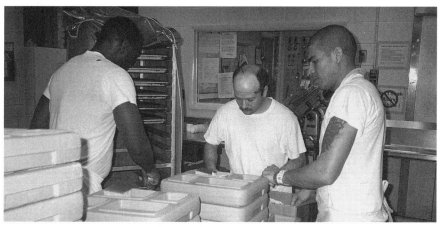

Many inmates earn good time and privileges by working in the jails' food service programs, laundry and janitorial sections.

who were on the educational staff of jails; and 12,000 individuals who were on the professional/technical staffs of jails.

A survey of 121 jails found that in 1994, the following services were offered:

Treatment	Jails	Average Number Per Day of Inmates Receiving Services
Detoxification	67	1,152
Education	102	3,028
Counseling: individual	83	1,330
Counseling: group	107	2,766
Therapeutic community	41	1,622
Community referrals	96	891

Source: Camp and Camp 1995

In 1995, 73.3 percent of United States jails classified inmates to ascertain appropriate constructive/rehabilitative programming (Camp and Camp 1995).

To supplement paid treatment staff, many jails use volunteers from the community who tutor, teach, and help with substance abuse programs, or help inmates close to release to link up with services in the community.

The following is an overview of jail treatment services and programs:

- **Self help substance abuse programs**: Groups such as Alcoholics Anonymous (AA), Narcotics Anonymous (NA), and Gamblers Anonymous conduct sessions in jails and show inmates positive ways to deal with problems through others who also have had trouble with alcohol, drugs, and gambling. These twelve-step groups work closely with the substance abuse staff.

- **Therapy**: Family therapy involves marriage counseling, improvement of parent-child relationships, and serves to strengthen ties with the family. Group therapy involves a trained therapist (psychiatrist, clinical psychologist, or other professional) who works with a small inmate group. Problems and solutions are explored; social skills are improved.

- **Counseling**: Counseling in jail involves developing a rapport or relationship between the inmate and counselor (vocational, mental health) so problems can be solved through mutual consent.

Inmates at the Dauphin County Prison in Pennsylavania, who participate in the Men Establishing New Directions (MENDS) program, learn how to change their attitudes and violent behavior toward women.

- **Educational**: A General Equivalency Diploma (GED) program allows inmates to obtain a high school equivalency diploma; Adult Basic Education (ABE) assists inmates who have less than a sixth-grade education.

In Orange County, Florida, jail inmates can choose between rehabilitation programs to learn skills to help them find and keep jobs after their release.

- **Religious**: Many jails have either a full-time chaplain or clergy member from the community to provide for the needs of inmates with various faiths through worship services, counseling, and family contacts.
- **Therapeutic Communities**: Therapeutic communities (TCs) treat offenders' problems by making a housing unit/cellblock an experiment in social living; inmates have to learn to live with others, use proper social skills, and to deal with their problems such as criminal thinking or substance abuse.

A varied recreation program can aid rehabilitative programing for inmates as well as reduce tension in the jail. Physical recreation includes basketball, volleyball, aerobics, or other activities. Other recreation includes games, television, radio, a leisure library with books and popular magazines. These allow inmates to use free time constructively, to improve physical and mental health, and to develop self-esteem, morale, and sportsmanship.

Recreation is important to inmates' morale and the release of tension.

Several examples of recent, innovative programs include:

- **Jails Anonymous (JA)**: modeled after Alcoholics Anonymous and Narcotics Anonymous philosophy and their twelve steps. Inmates in Jails Anonymous can deal with addiction to criminal behavior (Rushall 1995).
- **Jail Substance Abuse Program (JSAP)**: a three-phase program based in the Washington County (Maryland) Detention Center, JSAP is an institution-based treatment program emphasizing life skills, education, aftercare on release, and transition back to the community. From 1989 to 1994, 600 inmates completed the program at a taxpayer savings of almost $1 million (Brown and Messmer 1995).

The availability, size, number, and staffing of programs depends on commitment from the jail's administration and funds allotted or obtained by federal or state grants, or from other sources.

CHAPTER 9

Private Companies and Jails

One recent movement in corrections is that of "privatization"—the operation of correctional services by either nongovernmental profit or nonprofit organizations or private companies. These operations include private financing of construction/renovations, contract services such as health care, maintenance, or food service, or *total* management and operation of the facility. The goal of privatization is to reduce costs. Supporters of privatization believe that private companies provide better services cheaper than local government agencies, can cut through bureaucratic "red tape," hire and train more competent staff, and fire workers who do not do the job. Private correctional companies argue that they can provide more responsive staff and accessible, flexible programs at reduced cost (Allen and Simonsen 1995).

Private jails have a wide range of capacities and security levels. In Nashville, for example, the Metro Davidson County Detention Center, operated by Corrections Corporation of America, has a medium security level and a rated capacity of 1,092. The Odessa, Texas, Detention Center, run by the GRW Corporation, holds 100 in all security levels.

Jail inmate health care by private companies started about twenty years ago and has grown steadily. Rikers Island (New York) in 1973, Delaware County Prison (Pennsylvania) in 1978, and Clark County Jail (Nevada) in 1980 all contracted with local hospitals and health care services. Presently, 110 jails in twenty-five states are under private health care contract for an average daily population of 86,950 (Cotton 1995).

The issue of privatization of jails is hotly debated between the private and public sectors, and the outcome is not clear. Problem areas being examined include the following:

- quality assurance: opponents say that private companies may use "shortcuts" that could reduce the quality of personnel, services, and operations
- selectivity: what type of inmates would a private company house? Opponents of privatization feel that companies too often deal with low-risk, minimum-security inmates, and local governments are left

responsible for the management problems of violent and hard core inmates

- liability: privatization does not reduce liability for a county government. In the event of a suicide, inmate injury, or other problem, the government is ultimately responsible for contracting with the company and can be sued along with the private contractor

- appropriate roles: opponents argue that local corrections is a legislative obligation and private companies should not get involved with inmate discipline, use of force, parole recommendations, or good time policies. Others feel that corrections means control over a citizen's life and should not be turned over to a company for profit.

CHAPTER 10

Training of Jail Staff

To properly operate a jail—with all its problems—jail officers must be trained in a wide range of topics. Training standards for police and state correctional officers (COs) exist in virtually all states. Yet, in many states, lockup and jail officers are not included in training standards (Fox and Stinchcomb 1995).

In 1990, at least 120 hours of basic training for state correctional officers was required in almost all states; some states required more. In 1993, a study found a national average of 5.7 weeks of training for state correctional officers. A 1994 survey found that 143 jail systems required correctional officers to have an average of 282 hours of basic training, or about seven weeks (Stinchcomb 1995).

The American Correctional Association (ACA) correctional officers training standards call for a minimum of 120 hours of training during their first year of employment and 40 hours for each subsequent year (*1996 Standards Supplement*, "Adult Local Detention Facilities"). A 1984 survey conducted by the National Institute of Corrections (NIC) found that most states required only the minimum number of ACA hours.

This situation has improved with more jurisdictions increasing their training. Florida, Michigan, and Vermont require ten-to-sixteen weeks of training, and sixteen weeks of classroom training are required for local jail officers in Dade County, Florida.

Jail training does not occur just at the recruit level. In-service training is mandated by most states having training standards. In-service training requires officers to receive training (usually forty hours) yearly. Annual firearms training is normally required. Cross-training is necessary when staff transfer from one assignment to another (such as custody to classification).

Jail Training Curriculum

Generally, jail officer training is conducted through a training academy which must meet state standards. Training academies can serve their home jurisdictions or a regional academy may serve several jurisdictions. A state may combine police training and jail officer training so on graduation, the officer is certified both in law enforcement *and* corrections.

Jail training generally includes these subjects:
- Security procedures: key control, head counts, searches, and so on
- Inmate supervision
- Use of force regulations/procedures
- Report writing
- Inmate rules, regulations, discipline, due process
- Inmate rights and responsibilities
- Emergency procedures: fire, escape, hostages
- Weapons training: firearms, nonlethal weapons
- Defensive tactics
- Interpersonal communications/relations
- Inmate social/cultural lifestyle
- First aid/cardiopulmonary resuscitation
- Constitutional law and legal issues
- Ethics
- Driving
- Agency policies and procedures
- Suicide prevention
- Special management for inmates (mentally ill)
- On the job training

Source: American Correctional Association 1989, Fox and Stinchcomb 1994

In 1995, a survey of 130 jail systems by the Criminal Justice Institute reported an average requirement of 238 hours of pre-service training. Subsequently, an annual average of thirty-one hours of training were required (Camp and Camp 1995).

Many jails offer transition training to help officers from older jails be effective in direct supervision jails. The Hampden County, Massachusetts, sheriff's office developed a revolutionary training program for transition into their new facility. Using a training advisory committee, this department developed specialized training on the role of the officer and direct supervision (Canter 1995). In North Carolina, jail officers' training consists of a minimum of 135 hours on mandated topics including stress management, investigative duties of the jailer, and court testimony (Yearwood 1994). In Kansas, Washburn University offers courses to jail officers in basic jail operations and supervision and management. Students receive academic credit (Heim 1993). In Florida, Miami-Dade Community College offers computer-based training for criminal justice practitioners at its School of Justice and Safety Administration (Van Buren 1996).

A noteworthy improvement in jails is the training that has occurred in virtually all jails and prisons on AIDS education and in ways to handle tuberculosis, hepatitis, and other diseases.

CHAPTER 11

Problem Solving: Jails and the Community

Crowding, the need for new facilities, repeat offenders, strained budgets—these are a few of the problems facing our nation's jails. They cannot be solved alone—help from the community, the courts, and the police is needed.

Alternatives to Incarceration

Traditionally, placing an offender in pretrial detention or jail assured his or her appearance in court. However, other methods can be used to relieve crowding. These include nonfinancial release, financial release, and diversion programs.

Nonfinancial Release

- **Summons/citation**: An offender is given a summons to appear in court by the arresting officer.

- **Release on recognizance (ROR)**: The offender is released on a promise to appear in court. Certain criteria must be met—the offender must reside and work in the community, have no serious criminal record, have a good employment history, and meet other requirements.

- **Stationhouse release**: This is similar to release on recognizance. The offender is released at the police station or lockup after booking.

- **Conditional release**: The offender is released pending trial on the requirement that he or she meet certain requirements such as checking in with a pretrial release agency, maintaining residence, staying away from the victim and witnesses, and meeting other requirements.

- **Supervised release**: This is a step up from conditional release. The offender must participate in counseling, seek employment, and attend a substance abuse program.

- **Third-party release**: The offender is released to the custody of a relative, parent, friend, organization, halfway house, or treatment program who assume responsibility for the offender's court appearance.

Financial Release

- **Unsecured bail**: This is similar to release on recognizance. The offender is released on a bail amount set by the court. Offenders are held liable if they do not appear.
- **Deposit bail (also called 10 percent bail)**: The offender or others pay a percentage (generally 10 percent) of the face value of the bond to the court. After trial, offenders receive most of it back minus administrative fees.
- **Cash bail**: The offender must pay the full bail amount to secure release. If the offender makes the court appearance, the money is returned.
- **Surety bail**: The offender is released through services of a private bail bondsperson who posts bail and charges a fee which ranges from 5-20 percent. The bondsperson may require collateral.

Diversion Programs

Diversion programs divert the offender from the local jail by use of other resources in the community and criminal justice system. Diversion can happen at any time in the criminal justice process—until even adjudication or trial. For diversion programs to succeed, they need the cooperation of the police, courts, and community. Informal diversion techniques such as a verbal warning or referral to a social service agency are unofficial actions by which the police can remove the case from the criminal justice system.

Alternative dispute resolutions occur when the prosecutor decides not to file charges or offers to dismiss charges if the offender and victim work out a solution such as restitution for damages (for example, broken windows).

Formal diversion, or deferred prosecution, means that the case, while in the court system, can be disposed of if the offender meets certain conditions. If not, the case proceeds. Judges can withhold adjudication and divert the offender into community rehabilitative programs such as substance abuse education, vocational training, and family or mental health counseling. Judges, upon a finding of guilt, may suspend sentences and order offenders to participate in programs, thus keeping them out of jail.

TASC (Treatment Alternative to Street Crime) programs target drug offenders. Drug problems are diagnosed, and offenders are referred to treatment and monitored for progress (Fox and Stinchomb 1994). To remain diverted, the offender must follow the requirements set or face incarceration.

Groups Interacting with Jails

Many government officials and others can have an impact on local corrections. The following list cites examples of how each group can help their local jail:

- **Sheriffs/Jail administrators**:
  - inform judges daily of the jail population
  - improve contact with state legislators—request changes in laws or regulations that would offer alternatives to sentences, increased jail funding, and greater jail officer training
- **Probation officers**:
  - expedite the processing of presentence reports to the sentencing judge for jailed offenders
  - request use of community corrections and other alternatives to incarceration
- **Police**:
  - increase use of citations and summonses for minor offenders
  - divert special problem persons to community treatment programs
- **Judges/Court administrators**:
  - make greater use of alternatives to jail, pretrial release, diversion programs, third-party release, and other plans
  - speed up court proceedings
  - make magistrates available twenty-four hours per day, seven days per week for release decisions
  - expedite all court proceedings, whenever possible
  - provide enough intake staff who can screen out people inappropriate for jail (including the mentally ill) and place them in alternative programs such as a community treatment program
- **Public defenders/Defense attorneys**:
  - recommend alternatives to incarceration, especially for misdemeanors; make more use of community corrections

- **Prosecutors**:
  - recommend alternative sentences such as restitution or home detention
  - expedite court cases, specifically where inmates are awaiting trial or in mental disability cases
- **Pretrial release agencies**:
  - recommend increased use of release on recognizance and other nonfinancial forms of release
- **State legislators**:
  - enact legislation which establishes community corrections programs and allow the police to issue summonses or citations for misdemeanors
  - fund social service and local community mental health programs
  - establish state jail standards with enforcement clauses; provide financial aid to counties whose jails comply
- **Local officials**:
  - encourage alternatives to jail incarceration
  - establish planning groups, pretrial programs, and get input from all parts of the criminal justice system
  - fund social service programs for special needs inmates
- **Social service programs:**
  - make services available to special needs offenders, so that they may avoid jail; accept police referrals
  - provide twenty-four hour emergency services for the mentally ill; accept police referrals
  - provide training in identification and referral of special needs offenders to police and jail officers
- **Communities and Citizens**:
  - get educated about the local jails—who is incarcerated and for how long; visit or tour the jail
  - encourage the use of volunteers in treatment programs
  - encourage businesses to hire offenders in work release programs; make use of offenders in community service programs

Sheriffs and jail administrators must take a leading role in problem solving. All of these groups should participate on planning commissions to address problems such as crowding and funding.

CHAPTER 12

Future Trends in Jails

Things are improving in our nation's jails for the keepers and the kept.

Salaries for jail officers are improving. Jail officers' salaries depend on the size of the local jurisdiction and its revenues allocated for wages. On the average, officers' salaries started at $21,542.00, and the average maximum salary in 131 jails was $31,890 (Camp and Camp 1995).

Jails are hiring more staff. In 1993, an estimated 165,500 persons were employed by local jails. Total jail staff, including full time, part time, payroll and nonpayroll workers, increased 156 percent, or more than 100,000 from 1983 to 1993. Seventy percent of jail staff and 76 percent of jail officers are male. Female staff increased from 25,642 in 1988 to 48,000 in 1993. Between 1988 and 1993, the race and ethnic composition of jail staff remained unchanged. In 1993:

Total of paid staff

White employees:	69% of correctional officers
Black employees:	23% of correctional officers
Hispanic employees:	7% of correctional officers

Many jails offer a canteen where inmates can purchase food, over-the-counter medications, and personal hygiene items.

An increasing number of jails employ standards and receive accreditation. While jail standards exist in many state codes, accreditation of a jail by the American Correctional Association (ACA) improves operations, pride and morale, and enhances legal defensibility against litigation. ACA issues standards for not only personnel, fiscal issues, staffing, and similar administrative issues, they also cover:

- Physical plant
- Classification
- Custody and security
- Medical/health care
- Property control
- Library
- Activities/privileges for inmates
- Inmate discipline
- Food service
- Counseling, education, and recreation

Many jails offer programs in which the inmate can work independently, such as at the Clarke-Frederick-Winchester Regional Adult Detention Center in Virginia.

Over 800 correctional facilities have been involved in the accreditation process. As of 1996, there are 79 jails accredited by the American Correctional Association. Accredited facilities exist in forty-five states.

Community Corrections

Many researchers contend that innovative programs in community corrections provide solutions to jail crowding and foster rehabilitation of the inmate.

Community-based corrections refers to various types of noninstitutional or nontraditional programs for criminal offenders. Types of programs include: diversion, pretrial release, probation, restitution, community service, electronic monitoring, fine options, graduated/temporary release, halfway houses, work release, community service programs, parole, and inmate work programs. The goal of community-based corrections is to reintegrate offenders into the community, placing them back in the community as productive, responsible citizens. The community provides the offenders with resources to get help with their problems. The following are the most common types of community-based corrections programs in a jail setting:

- **Work release**: Inmates go to and from the facility and work in the community after being approved and meeting certain criteria—no detainers (charges pending in another jurisdiction), or no violent crimes within short time of release. Inmates may be court ordered or may apply and be screened. Participation in a treatment program may be required. The inmate pays room and board and is subject to alcohol/drug screenings and on-site community checks.

- **Home detention**: Inmates stay within their home. Frequently, this is used with electronic monitoring devices. The offender has to abide by conditions such as staying alcohol/drug free, participating in treatment programs, or paying restitution. Offenders who leave home to work and attend rehabilitative programs are charged a fee. Offenders wear a transmitter on their wrist or ankle which sends a signal over home telephone lines to the supervising office that they are home. A computer randomly may call the offender who must insert the transmitter into a device to send the signal. An estimated one in three offenders on home arrest wears a monitoring device. In early 1993, about 40,000 electronic monitors were in use. Some agencies use a voice-activated system that eliminates the need for hardware.

- **Day reporting centers:** Inmates on pretrial release, probation or parole are required to report to a center for participation in programs; failure to do so can result in revocation of their conditional release status.

- **Community service**: Offenders sentenced to community service perform work in the community—cutting grass in parks, cleaning schools, or doing other chores. Hours are worked off through cooperation with the local jail agency or the probation office supervisor.

- **Fine options**: Offenders under court order to pay a fine who are indigent may work the fine off through community service hours; the hourly rate is fixed by the correctional agency. (Example: $200.00 fine takes twenty hours to work off at a value of $10.00/hour.)

- **Work programs**: Many jurisdictions are taking selected, short time, nonviolent felons and misdemeanants and having them work in community park lands and on public properties. Inmates receive good time off their sentences.

- **Weekend confinement**: Offenders sentenced to jail confinement on weekends may be placed on work details with community service, fine options, or work programs.

- **Probation**: Straight probation is a sentence that does not place the offender in jail—instead conditions are imposed; the offender is supervised by a probation officer. If conditions are violated, the court may incarcerate or resentence the offender. Probationers are required to regularly report to the probation officer, stay drug free, keep a job, attend rehabilitative programs, and meet other probation conditions. They are subject to on-site home and job checks.

- **Shock probation**: Inmates are incarcerated for short periods of time and then placed on probation.

Boot Camps

Sometimes known as shock incarceration, "boot camps" started in Georgia (1983) and Oklahoma (1984). Most require inmates to volunteer, offering a short incarceration of several months, opposed to longer jail terms. Programs vary among local jurisdictions and state depart-

Boot camps are a growing option for jails.

ments of corrections, but basically target youthful offenders with a regimen of:

* military drills: calisthenics, barracks living
* military discipline
* physical labor
* specialized education/training/counseling
* substance abuse treatment

The goal is to give direction and discipline to offenders who have had none in their lives. Inmates can be placed on probation or in a community program after release (See American Correctional Association, *Juvenile and Adult Boot Camps* 1996).

Other Alternatives to Jail

Other alternatives to jail include: suspended sentences, fines, intensive supervised probation and similar options. All these options keep offenders out of jail and reserve cell space for extremely violent, hard core cases.

Concerning alternatives, 2,843,000 offenders were on probation in 1993. A study of 3,268 jails found the following data concerning alternatives in 1993 (Bureau of Justice Statistics 1995b).

Jails with no special program:	586
Jails operating only special program:	2,359

	Number of Jails	Inmate Participants
Work release	1,724	23,854
Weekend confinement	1,392	—
Community service	476	12,215
Electronic monitoring	300	4,259
Day reporting	134	1,516
Home detention	93	1,562
Other (drug/alcohol treatment, etc.)	55	7,582
Boot camp	50	1,196

Megajail Predictions

Megajail administrators predict in the next ten years (American Jail Association 1995):

– epidemics of AIDS and tuberculosis in jails
– expansion of jail industries
– diminishing revenues with which to fund jail operations
– increasing gang problems
– privatization
– increase in inmate programs
– continuing searches for alternatives to incarceration
– employee incentives
– inmate population becoming more institutionalized and sophisticated

Jail Information

For more information on jails in the United States contact:

The American Correctional Association
4380 Forbes Boulevard
Lanham, Maryland 20706-4322
1-800-ACA-JOIN — 301-918-1800

The American Jail Association
2053 Day Road, Suite 100
Hagerstown, Maryland 21740-9795
301-790-3930

The International Association
  of Correctional Training Personnel
2053 Day Road, Suite 100
Hagerstown, Maryland 21740-9795
301-790-3930

The National Institute of Corrections,
  Jail Center
1960 Industrial Circle, Suite A
Longmont, Colorado 80501
1-800-995-6429 — 303-682-0639

National Sheriffs' Association
1450 Duke Street
Alexandria, Virginia 22314-3490
703-836-7827

Glossary

Adjudication: process by which a court reaches a decision that terminates a criminal case or proceeding. It is a judgment, acquittal, or dismissal of that case.

Administrative segregation (AS): inmate is housed separately from the jail's general inmate population for other than disciplinary reasons, such as incompatibility with inmates, mental health reasons, at their own request, or any reason that calls for increased attention, surveillance, or supervision. In larger facilities, placement of an inmate on administrative segregation may be decided by an institutional classification committee rather than a staff person. The inmate receives the same privileges as the general inmate population, whenever possible.

Americans with Disabilities Act (ADA): a federal law passed by Congress in 1990 which guarantees access to employment opportunities, programs, and services to people with disabilities. Inmates with disabilities and their visitors must be provided access to any service, program, or activity that nondisabled inmates and visitors are provided.

Boot camp: shock incarceration program that combines military regimen with correctional rehabilitation philosophy; elements include military drill, physical exercise, labor, counseling, education, and substance abuse treatment.

Classification: assigning inmates to suitable living quarters based on risk factors such as criminal history, instant offense, behavioral characteristics. This section handles inmate problems, holds disciplinary hearings, and recommends programs.

Contraband: items not authorized by the jail administration (homemade weapons, illegal drugs), excess authorized items, or any item that is a threat to jail security.

Community corrections: programs that deal with offenders in the community: work release, home detention, probation/parole, diversion, pretrial release, fine options, community services, restitution.

County prison: another name for a jail.

CRIPA: Civil Rights of Institutionalized Persons Act. This federal law allows the Justice Department to sue a facility on behalf of inmates' civil rights and encourages development of grievance programs, 42 U.S.C. 1997.

Deliberate indifference: term used in civil rights litigation, defendants (jail staff) knew of serious conditions or problems and failed to respond and correct them.

Design capacity: number of inmates planned for by the architects and planners of the correctional facility.

Detainer: charge on a jail inmate from another jurisdiction; inmate will be extradited to that jurisdiction once current charge is adjudicated.

Detention center: another name for a jail.

Direct supervision: third generation jails where the officer is inside housing pod and acts as a behavior manager.

Disciplinary segregation: when an inmate is isolated as a result of serious violations of institutional rules and a finding of guilt after a due process disciplinary hearing. Privileges such as personal visiting, commissary, television, and programs may be suspended. The purpose is to punish wrongdoers and to isolate them from the general inmate population.

Diversion: officially stopping/suspending a case at any entry point in the criminal justice system, referral of offender to a treatment/care program, in lieu of further adjudication or incarceration.

Developmentally disabled inmates: inmates who have markedly lower intellectual capacity (IQ), lack social/life skills, or who are functionally illiterate, have learning disabilities, have organic brain disorders, or who are mildly retarded.

Due process: procedures that the state must afford a person facing deprivation of life, liberty, or property.

Emergency Response Team (ERT): selected correctional officers who are specially trained to handle emergencies including riots, assaultive inmates, large scale searches, and other concerns.

Federal Juvenile Justice and Delinquency Prevention Act: a 1974 federal law that established strict criteria and requirements on states that incarcerate juveniles in adult jails.

Felony: a criminal offense that is punishable by death or by incarceration in a state or federal prison, generally for one year or more. Violent felonies include: murder, rape, abduction, and robbery. See also Nonviolent felony.

First generation jails: see Linear jails.

General obligation bonds: method of financing jail construction. They usually carry a twenty-thirty year maturity at a fixed rate. They offer tax-exempt interest to investors. Voter approval often is required. These are paid back through property taxes.

House of correction: another name for a jail.

Jail: confinement facility operated by a local law enforcement agency, holding adults, and sometimes juveniles, pending trial or who have been sentenced to short terms of incarceration.

Jailhouse lawyer: an inmate who is knowledgeable in the law, usually self-taught, who helps other inmates with their cases or files lawsuits against the jail.

Linear jails: first generation jails where cells are aligned in rows.

Lockup: temporary holding facility, usually operated by a police department, that holds offenders pending bail or transport to jail; holds inebriates until ready for release or juveniles pending parent custody or shelter placement.

Misdemeanor: criminal offense, generally minor or petty, that is punishable by small fines or penalties or incarceration in a local jail for a year or less.

New generation jails: also known as direct supervision, correctional officer is stationed inside inmate housing unit without barrier. The goal is to positively manage inmate behavior.

Nonfinancial release: offender secures release from jail pending trial by promise to appear or be in custody of a third person; no money is paid to secure court appearance.

Nonviolent felony: criminal offense (see Felony) that did not involve injury or death to the victim nor violence in its commission. Nonviolent felonies include: burglary, grand larceny, embezzlement, and drug possession.

Operational capacity: the inmate population at which a jail can safely operate, usually decided by the administrator or agency head.

Parole: the process of releasing inmates from incarceration before the end of their sentence, on conditions of supervision by a parole officer and their maintenance of good behavior. If the conditions are violated, the offender will be reincarcerated.

Pretrial detainees: offenders awaiting trial, first court appearance, or for bail bond to be set.

Prisonization: the process by which an offender adapts to the culture of the inmate—how to get along, what inmates to avoid, which officers are helpful.

Privatization: private corporations either operating and managing the entire jail or providing certain services such as food, medical treatment, or maintenance.

Prison: adult confinement facility administered by a state or federal government, holding inmates for long sentences.

Probation: the release by the court of a convicted offender into the community with certain conditions, such as good behavior, under a suspended sentence. Offender is supervised by a probation officer. Shock probation involves incarcerating the offender for a short time, followed by probation.

Protective custody: placing inmates in administrative segregation for their protection, for example, as witnesses or informants.

Rated capacity: number of inmates or beds assigned to a jail by ratings officials such as a regional jail board or state department of corrections.

Recognizance: the release of an offender on his/her word of honor or promise to appear in court. The court is satisfied that the offender will appear and will not require the posting of bond or bail.

Regional jail: a local jail funded by several jurisdictions, usually operated by a jail board.

Reintegration: a model of treatment whose goal is to return the offender to the community as a productive citizen, who can handle problems using community resources.

Religious Freedom Restoration Act (RFRA): 42 U.S.C. 200bb, Public Law 103-141. A 1993 federal law that states that government (including correctional facilities) may not "substantially burden" a person's (including inmates) exercise of religion. Exceptions to this are to further a compelling government interest (such as security), and if so, must be done by the use of least restrictive means.

Second generation jails: the officer is in a control booth surrounded by inmates but has limited interaction with them.

Section 1983: informal term for 42 U.S.C. 1983, or the Civil Rights Act. Any person deprived of civil rights by persons acting under authority of law can pursue proceedings (such as a lawsuit) for redress.

Shock probation: See Probation.

Tax-exempt lease bonds: jail financing technique that raises capital quickly and source of lease payment must be identified. May be either variable or fixed rate.

Third generation jails: see Direct supervision.

Bibliography

Allen, Harry and Clifford Simonsen. 1992. *Corrections in America: 6th Ed.* New York: MacMillan.

———. 1995. *Corrections in America: 7th Ed.* Englewood Cliffs, New Jersey: Prentice Hall.

American Correctional Association. 1983. *Protective Custody in Adult Correctional Facilities: A Discussion of Causes, Conditions, Attitudes and Alternatives.* College Park, Maryland.

———. 1985. *Jails in America: An Overview of Issues.* College Park, Maryland.

———. 1989. *Correctional Officer Resource Guide.* Laurel, Maryland.

———. 1994. *Vital Statistics.* Laurel, Maryland.

———. 1996. *1996 Standards Supplement.* Lanham, Maryland.

———. 1996. *Juvenile and Adult Boot Camps:* Lanham, Maryland.

———. 1996. *Correctional Issues: Community Corrections.* Lanham, Maryland.

American Jail Association. 1993. Megajail Survey, Part III. *American Jails.* November- December, Vol. VII, No. 5, p. 12.

———. 1995. *American Jails.* November-December. Special issue devoted to special management inmates.

Atlas, Randall. 1995. ADA-Interim Final Rules for Courthouses, Jails, and Prisons. *The Keeper's Voice.* Winter, Vol. 16, No. 1, pp. 30-35.

Boston, John and Daniel Manville. 1995. *Prisoners' Self Help Litigation Manual: Third Edition.* New York: Oceana.

Boudouris, James, Ph.D. 1996. *Parents in Prison: Addressing the Needs of Families.* Lanham, Maryland: American Correctional Association.

Brown, Henry A. and Charles Messmer. 1995. Beyond the 90's—A Program that Works. *American Jails.* March-April, Vol. IX, No. 1, pp. 57-62.

Buie, James. 1993. Families, Police Protest Jailing of People Who Are Mentally Ill. *Advocate.* May, Vol. 14, No. 4.

Bureau of Justice Statistics. Special Report: *Profile of Jail Inmates, 1989.* April, 1991.

———. *Sourcebook of Criminal Justice Statistics.* 1994.

———. Bulletin: *Jails and Jail Inmates,* NCJ 151651. April, 1995b.

————. Bulletin: *Prisoners in 1994*. August, 1995c.

————. *Correctional Populations in the United States 1993*. October, 1995d.

Camp, Camille G. and George M. Camp.1995. *The Corrections Yearbook: 1995: Jail Systems*. South Salem, New York: Criminal Justice Institute.

Canter, Rosaling. 1995. Training is Good Operations: Operations is Good Training. *American Jails*. September-October, Vol. IX, No. 4, pp. 49-59.

Champion, Dean. 1990. *Corrections in the United States: A Contemporary Perspective*. Englewood Cliffs: Prentice Hall.

Charles, Michael, Ph.D., and Sesha Kethineni, Ph.D. 1992. The American Jail. *American Jails*. March-April, Vol. VI, No. 1, pp. 24-30.

Collins, William. 1993. *Correctional Law for the Correctional Officer*. Laurel, Maryland: American Correctional Association.

Collins, William and John Hagar. 1995. Jails and the Courts: Issues for Today, Issues for Tomorrow. *American Jails*. May-June, Vol. IX, No. 2, pp. 18-28.

Cornelius, Gary F. 1994. *Stressed Out: Strategies for Living and Working with Stress in Corrections*. Laurel, Maryland: American Correctional Association.

Corrections Professional. 1995. Supreme Court Alters Disciplinary Rules Landscape. August 25. 1:1, 4.

Cotton, Barbara. 1995. Privatization of Jail Health Care Services: The First Twenty Years. *American Jails*. January-February, Vol. VIII, No. 6, pp. 19-25.

Dale, Michael J. 1991. Children in Adult Jails: A Look at Liability. *American Jails*. January- February, Vol. IV, No. 5, pp. 28-31.

Drapkin, Martin. 1996. *Developing Policies and Procedures for Jails: A Step-by-Step Guide*. Lanham, Maryland: American Correctional Association.

Fisher, Margaret, et al. 1987. *Practical Law for Jail and Prison Personnel*. St. Paul, Minnesota: West Publishing Company.

Fox, Vernon and Jeanne Stinchcomb. 1994. *Introduction to Corrections, 4th Ed*. Englewood Cliffs: Prentice Hall.

Freeman, Robert. 1996. *Strategic Planning for Correctional Emergencies*. Lanham, Maryland: American Correctional Association.

Gonzales, Manuel A., Ph.D. 1994. Meeting the Educational Needs of Offenders in Northampton County, Pennsylvania. *American Jails*. July-August, Vol. VIII, No. 3. pp. 63-65.

Hansen, Roger and Henry W. K. Daley. 1995. *Challenging the Conditions of*

Prisons and Jails: A Report on Section 1983 Legislation. Bureau of Justice Statistics, January 1995.

Heim, Ted. 1993. The University's Role in Training Jail Personnel. *American Jails*. March-April, Vol. VII, No. 1, pp. 18-20.

Jackson, P. G. 1991. Competing Ideologies of Jail Confinement. In Thompson and Mays, eds. *American Jails –Public Policy Issues*. Chicago: Nelson Hall.

Jefferis, Eric. 1994. Violence in Correctional Institutions. *American Jails*. September-October, Vol. VIII, No. 4, pp. 25-32.

Jones, Wendy R. 1995. Working With the Developmentally Disabled in Jail. *American Jails*. November-December, Vol. IX, No. 5, pp. 16-20.

Judiscak, Daniel. 1995. Why Are the Mentally Ill in Jail. *American Jails*. November-December, Vol. IX, No. 5, pp. 9-15.

Kerle, Ken, Ph.D. 1991. Juveniles and Jails. *American Jails*. January-February, Vol. IV, No. 5, p. 3.

―――. 1994. Jails: The Growing TB Menace. *American Jails*. March-April, Vol. VIII, No. 1, p. 5.

McCarthy, Belinda and Bernard J. McCarthy. 1991. *Community-Based Corrections: Second Edition*. Pacific Grove, CA: Brooks-Cole.

National Institute of Justice. 1986. Ohio's New Approach to Prison and Jail Financing. *Construction Bulletin*. November.

―――. 1996: Survey of Jail Administrators. May.

Ness, James, Ph.D. 1996. Preparing and Training for Jail Emergencies. *American Jails*. January- February, Vol. IX, No. 6, pp. 37-42.

Ragghianti, Marie. 1994. Save the Innocent Victims of Prison. *Parade*. February 6, 1994, p. 14.

Ray, Oakley and Charles Ksir. 1992. *Drugs, Society and Human Behavior, 6th Ed*. St. Louis: Mosby Yearbook.

Rowan, Joseph. 1991. *Suicide Prevention in Custody*, Intensive Study Course. Laurel, Maryland: American Correctional Association.

Rubin, Paula and Susan McCampbell. *The Americans With Disabilities Act and Criminal Justice: Providing Inmate Services*. National Institute of Justice Research in Action, July 1994.

―――. *The Americans with Disabilities Act and Criminal Justice: Mental Disabilities and Corrections*. National Institute of Justice Research in Action, September, 1995.

Rushall, Judith. 1995. 12 Steps to a Crime Free Life. *American Jails*. March-

April, Vol. IX, No. 1, pp. 42-44.

Smith, Robert R., M.D. 1994. TB Crisis in Our Nation's Jails. *American Jails*. March-April, Vol. VIII, No. 1, pp. 11-14.

Stinchcomb, Jeanne, Ph.D. 1995. Breaking with Tradition . . . Linking Correctional Training and Professionalism. *American Jails*. September-October, Vol. IX, No. 4, pp. 49-59.

Thompson, Arthur P. and Wesley Ridlon. 1995. How ADA Requirements Affect Small Jail Design. *Corrections Today*. April. 57:2.

Thompson, Joel and G. Larry Mays, eds. 1991. *American Jails: Public Policy Issues*. Chicago: Nelson Hall.

Trupin, Eric, Ph.D., Susan Rahman, M.S., and Ron Jemelkea, Ph.D. 1993. Mentally Ill Offenders: The Need for Incarceration Alternatives. In *The State of Corrections*. Laurel, Maryland: American Correctional Association.

Van Buren, William T. 1996. Computer-Based Training. *American Jails*. January-February, Vol. IX, No. 6, pp. 19-22.

Vandenbraak, Sarah. No Room at the Jail. *USA Today*. August 17, 1995, p. 11A.

Veysey, Bonita M., et al. Double Jeopardy: Persons with Mental Illnesses in the Criminal Justice System: A Report to Congress, February 24, 1995. Rockville, Maryland: Center for Mental Health Services.

Virginia Department of Mental Health and Mental Retardation. Office of Forensic Services. *Mental Health Education for Police, Jail, and Mental Health Professionals Trainer's Manual,* Sections II, III, and IV. Joseph Rowan, Project Consultant. Frank Patterson, Project Director. June 1986.

Welsh, Wayne, Matthew Leone, Patrick Kinkade and Henry N. Pontell. 1991. The Politics of Jail Overcrowding: Public Attitudes and Official Policies. In Thompson and Mays, eds. *American Jails: Public Policy Issues*. Chicago: Nelson Hall.

Yearwood, Douglas. 1994. Jail Officer Training in North Carolina. *American Jails*. September-October, Vol. VIII, No. 4, pp. 53-59.